Forest Animals

By Christopher Butz

Raintree Steck-Vaughn Publishers

A Harcourt Company

Austin · New York

www.raintreesteckvaughn.com

Published by Raintree Steck-Vaughn Publishers, an imprint of Steck-Vaughn Company.

Library of Congress Cataloging-in-Publication Data
Butz, Christopher
    Forest animals / Christopher Butz.
        p. cm. -- (Animals of the biomes)
    Summary: Describes the physical characteristics, behavior, adaptations, and life cycle of four forest animals: the red-shouldered hawk, praying mantis, red deer, and king cobra.
    Includes bibliographical references (p.).
    ISBN: 0-7398-5687-1 (hc); 0-7398-6407-6 (pbk).
        1. Forest animals--Juvenile literature. [1. Forest animals.] I. Title. II. Series.
QL112 .B895 2002
591.73--dc21

2002069711

Printed and bound in the United States of America
1 2 3 4 5 6 7 8 9 10 WZ 05 04 03 02 01

Produced by Compass Books

Photo Acknowledgments
Claudia Adams, cover, 45; Comstock, 2; Charlie Heidecker, 8, 11, 44; Corbis, 30; Joe McDonald, 13, 18, 24, 27, 28, 32, 44, 45; William J. Weber, 14; Robert Domm, 16; Lindholm, 20; Sharon Gerig, 23; Ken Lucas, 35; Jeff Foot, 36; A. B. Sheldon, 39; Digital Stock; 40, 42.

Content Consultant
Dr. Jane Packard
Department of Wildlife and Fisheries Sciences, Texas A&M University
College Station, TX

This book supports the National Science Standards.

Contents

This red-shouldered hawk is one of many animals that live in forest trees.

Animals in the Forest

The forest biome is one that contains many trees. A biome is a large region, or area, made of communities. A community is a group of certain plants and animals that live in the same place.

Animals and plants that live in the forest have adapted to live in and among the trees. To adapt means that something changes over time to adjust to conditions, such as climate, in a specific area. Climate is the usual weather of an area.

The three main kinds of forest are coniferous forest, deciduous forest, and tropical rain forest. Each type of forest has different plants, trees, and animals living there.

Arctic Ocean

Europe

Asia

North
America

Atlantic
Ocean

Pacific
Ocean

Africa

South
America

Indian
Ocean

Australia

N
W E
S

Mix of Deciduous and Coniferous Forests
Coniferous Forest
Rain Forest
Oceans
Continents

This map shows where forests are located around the world.

What Lives in Forests?

Conifers are the most common trees in coniferous forests. Conifers, such as pine trees, grow cones and have needles instead of leaves. Coniferous forests grow best in cold places.

Deciduous forests are named for the **deciduous** trees, such as maples and birches, that grow there. Deciduous trees have leaves that change color. The leaves fall off in autumn and grow back in spring. These forests grow in areas with mild temperatures, where rain or snow falls throughout the year.

Tropical rain forests make up half of the forest biome across the world. These forests grow in hot and rainy tropical places near the equator. The equator is an imaginary line that circles Earth.

Many kinds of animals live in the forests as well. Some kinds of animals in coniferous forest have thick fur to help them adapt to the cold. Other kinds of animals in deciduous forests hibernate to help them save energy during winter. To hibernate is to spend the winter in a sleep-like state.

In the next chapters, you will learn about four forest animals. Red-shouldered hawks are birds that hunt. Praying mantises are insects that eat other insects. Red deer live in the forests of Europe and Asia. King cobras are snakes that live in some Asian rain forests. Keep reading to find out how each of these animals has adapted to live in its forest home.

You can see the reddish patch of feathers on this red-shouldered hawk.

The Red-Shouldered Hawk

The red-shouldered hawk is a raptor. A raptor hunts other animals for food. All raptors have hooked beaks and sharp claws called **talons**.

Red-shouldered hawks are medium-sized raptors. They range from 18 to 20 inches (46 to 51 cm) long from the head to the tip of the tail. Males weigh 19 to 20 ounces (540 to 570 mg), while females weigh 24 to 25 ounces (680 to 710 mg).

The tops of the red-shouldered hawk's wings, or shoulders, are reddish. The rest of the wings are dark brown with black and white stripes. Its head and back are brown, while its chest is white with light brown streaks. The tail is brown with white bands and a white tip.

Where Do Red-Shouldered Hawks Live?

Red-shouldered hawks live in lowland forests throughout the eastern half of the United States and in California and Mexico. They usually live near water.

Most red-shouldered hawks live in large trees in deciduous forests. They build nests in the crooks of these trees. A crook is the place where a thick branch grows from the tree trunk. Red-shouldered hawks build their nests mostly of twigs and bark. Then they line the inside of the nests with soft plants and feathers.

Red-shouldered hawks have home ranges of 4 square miles (10 sq km) or larger. They fly around their home ranges to search for food. They often have several perches throughout their home ranges. A perch is a place high in the trees that offers a clear view of the surrounding land.

How Have Red-Shouldered Hawks Adapted to Live in the Forest?

The red-shouldered hawk has adapted to its forest home in different ways. Those that live in warmer southern areas stay in the same forest all year round, but red-shouldered hawks that

These red-shouldered hawks are on a perch in a tall tree.

live in colder deciduous forests **migrate**. Migrate means to move from place to place with the seasons. Red-shouldered hawks go south to find food and water during winter. They return north during summer, when food and water are easy to find. In the summer, they may travel as far north as the forests of southern Canada.

What a Red-Shouldered Hawk Eats

Red-shouldered hawks are **carnivores**. Carnivores eat only the flesh of other animals. Common foods for the red-shouldered hawk are toads, frogs, small fish, crawfish, insects, squirrels, mice, rats, birds, and snakes. They also eat small birds, such as bluebirds and sparrows.

The red-shouldered hawk has special hunting abilities. It has excellent eyesight. This helps it spot small prey moving on the forest floor, even from high perches. Its strong talons grip prey tightly, and its strong wings help it fly the prey back to its perch to eat. Red-shouldered hawks can grab a small animal and carry it away, even if the prey is holding onto branches.

Like other birds, red-shouldered hawks do not have teeth. Instead, its beak is pointed and bends down sharply at the tip. This helps the hawk tear the prey into little pieces. Once the meal is torn into small pieces, the hawk swallows the pieces whole.

Because they have no teeth, red-shouldered hawks have a special part to help them **digest**. Digest means to break down food so the body

This red-shouldered hawk is eating small pieces of prey that it has caught.

can use it. This body part is called a gizzard. Red-shouldered hawks swallow small stones and other rough objects. These rough objects stay in the gizzard. Food rubs against these objects and breaks down into smaller pieces. This helps the red-shouldered hawk turn its food into energy that its body can use.

This red-shouldered hawk chick is covered with fluffy down feathers.

A Red-Shouldered Hawk's Life Cycle

Red-shouldered hawks mate in the early spring. To find mates, they fly in circles high above the trees. They also call to each other with loud whistles and screams.

The female lays two to four white, brown-spotted eggs in late March or early April. Both parents take turns sitting on the eggs. This incubates the eggs. To **incubate** is to keep eggs warm so the young animals can grow inside. If the eggs become too cold, the baby hawks will die.

After about 28 days, the baby red-shouldered hawks hatch. Newly hatched red-shouldered hawks are called chicks. Chicks are covered with soft white feathers called down. Until their flying feathers grow, chicks cannot fly. For about five weeks, the parents must feed the young chicks.

After about 45 days, their flying feathers will have grown. The chicks become fledglings when they make their first flight out of the nest. For about ten weeks, the young hawks stay with their parents. They learn how to fly and hunt. Then they leave to find their own home range.

The long body and extra-long front legs of this praying mantis are shown here.

The Praying Mantis

The praying mantis is an insect. An insect has six legs and a body that is divided into three sections. These three sections are the head, thorax, and abdomen.

Praying mantises have triangle-shaped heads with large eyes. Their bodies are long. Unlike other insects, praying mantises have very long, jointed front legs with spines on them. They also have two pairs of wings. They have two antennae, which they use to smell and feel with.

Praying mantises are different sizes and colors. Most praying mantises range in length from less than 0.5 inch (1.3 cm) to more than 6 inches (15 cm). They can be different colors, ranging from brown to green.

The green color of this praying mantis helps it blend in with the leaves.

Where Do Praying Mantises Live?

There are about 2,000 different kinds of praying mantis. They live in many parts of the world. Most kinds of mantis live in the tropical rain forests. Other kinds of mantis are common in the deciduous forests of North America, Europe, and Asia.

How Have Praying Mantises Adapted to Live in the Forest?

The coloring and shape of the mantis provide camouflage. Camouflage is colors, shapes, and patterns that make something blend in with its background. Camouflage makes it hard for **predators** to find praying mantises. A predator is an animal that hunts another animal as food. Birds and bats will eat praying mantises. Many mantises that live in rain forests are pink or other bright colors. This camouflage helps them blend in with the flowers and fruits around them. Praying mantises in deciduous forests are usually brown or green. This makes them blend in with twigs and leaves.

The head of the praying mantis is also very different from other insects' heads. The praying mantis is the only insect that can turn its head 180 degrees. The mantis's two compound eyes can see movement up to 60 feet (18 m) away. In between the two compound eyes, the mantis has three simple eyes on its forehead. Scientists believe that these eyes just sense light and darkness.

This praying mantis is eating an insect that it has caught.

What a Praying Mantis Eats

A praying mantis is a carnivore and will eat almost anything it catches. Insects are a mantis's most common food. They also eat other praying mantises.

Praying mantises have adapted to be good hunters. The thorax of the mantis is very long and can twist back and forth. This means the mantis can turn its head and upper legs without moving its body. This helps it spot prey.

The praying mantis's powerful front legs are also important to hunting. The front legs are divided into three sections. The front section folds back neatly against the middle section. Both these sections have sharp spines on the inside.

When hunting, the praying mantis waits until the prey moves close. Then the mantis reaches out with its front legs and grabs the prey. The mantis closes the front and middle sections of its legs around its prey. The mantis's strong grip presses its small spines into the prey and holds it tightly. Then the mantis pulls the prey to its mouth.

Like other insects, the mantis does not have teeth. Instead, it has a pair of sharp pincers called mandibles. It uses its mandibles to crush and tear its food as it eats.

When it has finished eating, the mantis cleans itself. It carefully nibbles on its front legs with its mandibles.

The Life Cycle of the Praying Mantis

Most insects have four life stages—egg, larva, pupa, and adult. Praying mantises and a few other insects go through a different life cycle. Their life cycle has only three stages. They start out as eggs, like all insects. When they hatch, however, they already look like adults, only smaller. In this stage, they are called nymphs. Then they grow larger, until they are adults.

In the autumn, the adult mantises mate. Right after mating, the female finds a twig or a leaf. There she creates an egg case by releasing a foamy material from her abdomen. She lays up to 400 eggs inside the foam. Within a few hours, the foam hardens into a shell-like covering. This covering helps keep the eggs warm through winter. The male and female die soon after mating.

When it becomes warmer, the eggs begin to develop into young mantises. By May or June, the little mantises hatch. They are then known as nymphs. Nymph mantises are pale green and easy to see when they first hatch. Predators eat most nymphs before they grow to be adults.

This praying mantis is laying eggs inside a foamy covering.

All insects have a hard outer covering called an exoskeleton. It does not become larger when the insect does. In order to grow, a nymph must shed its exoskeleton in a process called molting. Nymph mantises molt several times. With each molt, the mantis grows larger. Its wings also get bigger until the mantis is fully grown.

The antlers of this male red deer can be used for protection. Only males grow antlers.

The Red Deer

Red deer are large, four-legged mammals. A mammal is a warm-blooded animal with a backbone. Female mammals give birth to live young and feed them with milk from their bodies. Warm-blooded animals have a body temperature that stays the same, no matter what the temperature of the air or water around them.

Red deer are named for their color. Their coat is dark red or brown. They have white on their belly, inner legs, and backside.

Like all deer, red deer have long, thin legs with strong muscles. They walk on their two middle toes, which form a tough divided hoof. Red deer also have long, thin necks, big ears, and large, round eyes. Males grow antlers.

Where Do Red Deer Live?

Red deer live in many different places around the world. Many live in the cold evergreen coniferous forests of England, Scotland, central and eastern Europe, Asia Minor, central Asia, Siberia, China, and New Zealand.

Red deer have a home range of 1 mile (2.6 km) or larger. They travel around their ranges to look for food. Their range usually includes meadows in forested areas. The deer can find many different kinds of food there.

Red deer are social animals. This means that they live together in groups. Usually the males stay in their own groups, and the females and their young form other groups. Only during mating season do males live with the females.

How Have Red Deer Adapted to Live in the Forest?

Red deer have adapted to live in different kinds of forest. The colder the area where the red deer live, the bigger the deer normally are. This is because it is easier for a bigger animal to keep its body heat. The farther north the red

 This red deer is resting in its home range.

deer live, the bigger they grow. This helps them survive during cold northern winters.

Living in forests also helps red deer keep warm. The trees help block the cold wind. Red deer have a double coat of fur. This extra fur helps them hold in body heat.

These red deer are eating grass. Red deer
spend up to one-half of their day grazing.

What a Red Deer Eats

Red deer are herbivores. Herbivores eat only
plants. Red deer usually graze in grassy, open
fields. They eat grasses and leaves from shrubs.

Red deer graze only for short periods of time.
To graze is to feed on growing grasses. While
grazing, the deer's head is close to the ground.

Because of this, the red deer has a hard time seeing, hearing, or smelling nearby predators. To stay safe while grazing, the red deer eats for a short time, then brings its head up to check for danger. Then it wanders away to another grazing spot. This makes it hard for a predator to sneak up on the deer. Wolves, lynx, and bears will eat red deer if they can catch them.

Red deer are ruminants. A ruminant has four stomachs and a different way of digesting food than other mammals.

When the red deer eats, its food enters the first stomach and begins to digest. Then the deer regurgitates its food. To regurgitate is to bring the food back up out of its stomach into its mouth. After regurgitating, the red deer chews its food again for several minutes. This is called chewing its cud.

After it is finished chewing its cud, it swallows the chewed-up ball of partly digested food again. This passes into its second stomach. From there, it goes into the third and fourth stomachs, which finish the digestion. By doing this, the red deer receives energy from grasses and leaves that other mammals could never live on.

The white spots on the back of this sleeping fawn will disappear when it gets older.

The Life Cycle of the Red Deer

Red deer have a six-week mating season that begins in September. The mating season is also called the rutting season. During mating season, the bucks leave their groups to look for does. Usually one buck will try to find a small group of does to mate with.

A buck will fight other males that try to mate with the does he has found. Usually only bucks of the same size will fight. Smaller bucks will turn away. When bucks fight, they lower their heads and run toward each other. They smash their antlers against each other's until one of them pushes the other away. Males that earn the right to mate with females are from 5 to 11 years old. Older deer are usually stronger and larger, so they win the fights.

About eight months after mating, the does give birth to fawns. Fawns look like their parents, except that they have little white spots on their backs. Fawns stand up and begin walking within an hour of birth. They drink milk from their mothers and stay near them. Mothers and fawns know each other by scent. A doe will allow only her own fawn to drink milk from her.

FUN FACT

Red deer have a very good sense of hearing. With their large ears, deer can often hear predators before seeing them. They can also smell predators that are hiding. The deer will run if they sense danger.

This king cobra is showing its hood. It does this by spreading the ribs in its neck.

The King Cobra

The king cobra is the largest venomous snake in the world. A venomous animal poisons other animals by biting, touching, or spitting at them. King cobras are mainly about 12 feet (3.7 m) long, but some grow up to 18 feet (5.5 m) long. They have 0.5-inch (1-cm)-long fangs.

King cobras are different colors, depending on where they live. They are usually olive, gray, brown, or black. Their eyes are bronze colored.

Like all snakes, king cobras are covered with scales. A scale is a small piece of thick, tough skin. They also have long ribs in their neck. The king cobra spreads these ribs when it senses danger. The spread ribs create a hood around the neck that makes the snake look larger.

Where Do King Cobras Live?

King cobras live only in Asia. They live in many different countries, including Malaysia, Indonesia, Vietnam, India, and the Philippines.

Because they are cold-blooded, wild king cobras live only in warm tropical forests. Cold-blooded animals have a body temperature that changes depending on the outside temperature. Cobras need to keep warm to survive. They will die if they become too cold. Their common home is in rain forests. There, they live near streams in the undergrowth. The undergrowth is made up of the shrubs and small trees that grow on the rain forest floor.

How Have King Cobras Adapted to Live in the Forest?

King cobras have adapted coloring to help them survive in their homes. King cobras that live in thick forests usually have darker skins than those that do not. The dark color helps them blend in with the shade provided by the trees. King cobras that live in lightly forested places have lighter skins. In these places, dark skin would make them easier to see.

▲ **This king cobra has its eyes open to keep watch for enemies.**

King cobras have developed sharp senses to help them find and catch prey in forests. They can see prey moving from as far as 300 feet (91 m) away. At night, they can sleep with their eyes open. This helps them spot prey or any enemies. Wild boar and mongoose may kill and eat small king cobras.

 This king cobra is eating another snake.
King cobras' main food is other snakes.

What a King Cobra Eats

King cobras are carnivores. Their Latin name is *Ophiophagus hannah*, which means snake-eater. The king cobras received this name because their most common food is snakes. They eat rat snakes, krait snakes, and other kinds of cobras, including other smaller king cobras.

To eat, king cobras first must find prey. They do this mainly by their sense of smell. King cobras use their Jacobson's organ to smell. This organ is like a nose inside the top of the snake's mouth. To smell, the king cobra flicks its tongue in and out of its mouth. When the tongue is outside the mouth, it picks up scents in the air. When inside the mouth again, the tongue passes the scents to the Jacobson's organ.

After finding prey, they bite it with their hollow fangs. When the king cobra bites, venom passes through its fangs into the prey. Venom is a natural poison made inside some animals' bodies. The venom kills the prey.

King cobras do not have teeth for chewing or tearing prey. Their fangs only inject venom. King cobras must swallow their meals whole. First, their venom begins to break down the food. Then, as the king cobra swallows prey, it also bites into the meal with its back teeth. These teeth poke holes into the skin. As the meal passes into the stomach, digestive juices flow into these small holes. This helps the king cobra break down its food more quickly.

A King Cobra's Life Cycle

King cobras do not have a special mating season. When they are ready to mate, king cobras release a special musky scent from their body. Other male and female cobras can sense this scent. They travel toward the scent until they find each other. After mating, the female can produce eggs for several years.

King cobras are the only snakes that build nests. The female does this once the eggs have started to develop inside of her. To build a nest, she gathers a large pile of leaves together with her body. The nest has two levels. She lays 20 to 40 eggs in the lower level. Then the female stays in the upper level to guard the eggs.

After about two months, the eggs hatch. When they begin hatching, the mother leaves. Some scientists think she leaves so that she will not eat her young. The newly hatched king cobras are black with bright yellow stripes. They are only about 14 inches (35 cm) long.

Snake scales do not grow. Because of this, the growing snake must shed its skin. The newly

> ▲ The bright yellow stripes on this young king cobra will fade as it grows older.

hatched king cobras shed once a month during their first year. After that, they shed four to six times each year. When a king cobra sheds its skin, there is a new, larger skin underneath. The king cobra also grows a new tongue and new fangs every time it sheds.

If too many trees are cut down, animals such as this deer will have nowhere to live.

What Will Happen to Forest Animals?

Forests provide a special habitat for the animals that live there. Many plants and animals that live in forests could not live in other biomes.

Over time, people have begun to change forests. Deciduous and coniferous forests are major sources of wood. Wood is important for building houses and making furniture. If a forest is near a growing city, its trees will often be cut down to make room for more people.

Tropical rain forests are in the greatest danger. Often the forest gets cut down because farmers need the land to grow food for their families. People sometimes cut down trees to create huge farms that grow beans, bananas, or sugarcane.

> The red deer population is healthy because laws limit hunting.

How Are Forest Animals Doing?

Some animals of the forests have healthy populations. A population is the total number of one kind of animal. Praying mantises, red-shouldered hawks, and red deer are forest animals that are doing well. People hunt red deer for food. But there are laws that limit the number of red deer that hunters can kill. Because there are so many deer, this limited hunting is not a threat to the red deer population.

However, some animals of the forest are **endangered**. Endangered means an animal is close to becoming **extinct**, or dying out entirely, in the wild. When the forests are cut down, the habitats of forest animals become smaller. Animals that once lived over a large area are found in fewer places. This is happening to the king cobra. Once, the king cobra was a common snake in India. Many forests in India have been cut down to make room for people and cities. Today, there are very few wild king cobras living there.

People must feed their families and have places to live, but the forests are important, too. The trees release oxygen into the air and help keep the water clean. They also are home for thousands of different animals and millions of different insects.

To keep Earth healthy, we must find new ways to meet the needs of people while still protecting the forests. This way, forest animals can live safely in their homes for a long time.

Quick Facts

The red-shouldered hawk is a member of the family of birds that includes hawks, eagles, and kites. They are all birds of prey, which means they hunt animals for food.

The praying mantis got its name because the tips of its front legs bend over when it rests. This makes it look like it is praying. Because it is such a fierce hunter, it is also sometimes called the preying mantis.

Red deer are not as active during winter. Also, their bodies use energy more slowly in winter than they do in summer. This helps them save energy.

King cobras cannot see different colors, only black and white.

The venom of every type of cobra is strong enough to kill a person with a single bite.

Glossary

carnivores (KAHR-nuh-vorz)—animals that eat only meat

conifers (KON-uh-furz)—evergreen trees that produce cones

deciduous (di-SIJ-oo-uhss)—trees that shed their leaves each year

digest (dye-JEST)—to break down food so the body can use it as energy

endangered (en-DAYN-jurd)—a plant or animal species that is in danger of dying out

extinct (ek-STINGKT)—when all of one kind of animal or plant has died out in the wild

incubate (IN-kew-bate)—to sit on eggs so that body heat will help young animals grow inside the eggs

migrate (MYE-grate)—to move from place to place by season or in search of food

predators (PRED-uh-turz)—animals that hunt other animals for food

talons (TAHL-unz)—long, sharp claws on a raptor's feet

Addresses and Internet Sites

American Forests
P.O. Box 2000
Washington, D.C. 20013

USDA Forest Service
P.O. Box 96090
Washington, D.C. 20090

Educational in Nature:
  Forests
www.gp.com/Educational
inNature/topics/index.
html

Live from the Rainforest
passporttoknowledge.com
/rainforest/intro.html

The Wonderful World of
  Trees
www.domtar.com/arbre/
english/start.htm

USDA For Kids
www.usda.gov/news/
usdakids/

Books to Read

Miller, Chuck.
  Forest Scientists.
  Austin, TX:
  Steck-Vaughn, 2002.

Nelson, Julie.
  Forests. Austin, TX:
  Steck-Vaughn, 2001.

Index